ALEXIS GREIG

Business Building For Beginners

The Inspirational Guide To Equip Your New Way To Make Money

First edition

This book was professionally typeset on Reedsy.
Find out more at reedsy.com

Contents

1

Introduction

Welcome to the beginning of a new mindset, a milestone that can shape your life and the lives of your loved ones. While there are countless manuals and guidebooks for your specific business idea, this guide is designed to help you change your direction, find inspiration, and determine your desired path.

If you've picked up this book, you've already contemplated an alternative way to earn a living, and it all starts with your mind. Before we embark on this journey, consider a few questions:

What circumstances or events in your life have led you to consider working for yourself?

Since you hold the power to change your income, are you willing to do whatever it takes (within reason) to improve it?

How will this transformation positively impact your life and the lives of those around you?

What might happen if you don't embark on this new chapter?

I grew up in a city where being trapped in a system and a particular mindset was the norm. I wasn't the brightest student in school by far, and I only attended college because of a promise I made to my dad. Even during middle and high school, some of my friends became parents at a young age or got involved in substance abuse, much like their parents or others in their environment. While my parents stood out among their group of friends, they too were caught in a cycle, pursuing careers out of necessity and with limited access to opportunities at the time. The good news is that the present offers countless possibilities for those willing to embrace a new way of thinking.

As you read this book, I encourage you to journal/take notes, engage in prayer or reflection, and allocate at least an hour each day to implementing any necessary changes. Now, let's embark on the first chapter of your new life...

2

Start To Dream

"The secret of getting ahead is getting started."
Mark Twain, American Writer and Publisher

Many of us grew up being told that we had to fit into a list of roles. And to be honest, I was so sad when I got to college and spoke with my counselor who listed off careers for me to consider. I felt duped, in shock that life would amount to just finding a spot in line until we get old enough to retire, then barely afford to live on social security, then die. That was such a depressing thought to me! Now don't get me wrong- we need certain roles in our society to take care of the majority. However, so many of these roles and models can be altered to provide what is needed but in better ways.

I grew up with my mom working as a childcare provider in our home, dedicating long hours to make a good income. However, she rarely had the time to enjoy other things she was interested in and the flexibility she desired. After college, I found myself in need of income and asked if I could work for her, having previously helped out during high school. At that point, she had expanded to a larger location but still carried most of the workload. After about a year, it became clear to me that she was stuck in a cycle that would be difficult to break free from, and the thought of her continuing like this until retirement frightened me. I realized that I could delve deep into the business, learning every aspect of it, and hopefully alleviate much of her burden. However, I eventually understood that my thinking was limited. My initial goal was simply to lighten her load, without considering the bigger picture.

Fast forward, and there I was, marrying the love of my life - feeling incredibly honored to tie the knot with my best friend. As time went on, he began observing my actions, and before I knew it, he asked a question that would change our lives forever: "Would you be willing to create our very own childcare program?" Initially, I was hesitant. I didn't want to find myself trapped in the same cycle as my mom, despite the allure of financial stability. I had personal goals and passions that I yearned to pursue. However, as a young married couple, we knew we needed to increase our income to escape the cycle of living paycheck to paycheck.

One thing my husband said truly resonated with me - we didn't have to follow the same blueprint I witnessed growing up. We could imitate the good things and reimagine the elements we wished to see change. To keep a long story short, we took a small step, starting within our own home. We created systems that established our unique brand, eagerly seeking input from our first group of families. We focused on excellence, making the most of what we had. Within three years, we expanded, owning two more facilities while expanding our original location. We took on the responsibility of managing and administering my mom's program. We even appointed her as the Executive Director, overseeing the training of our directors and their teams, among other things that she enjoyed being a part of. This arrangement allowed her to have a more flexible schedule, which was our goal, and also resulted in increased income. Ultimately, the new setup proved to be beneficial for all parties involved, a true win-win situation.

At one point, we were running a total of five childcare centers, with thoughts of expanding further. We employed over 20 individuals, while my husband and I worked remotely, 300 miles away from our centers. Our team comprised of valuable teachers, directors, and our assistant administrator, doing what they each loved to do. Rather than spending money on formal education, much of our success came from recognizing the needs of others and taking the bold risks necessary to fulfill them. It is a tremendous honor to provide employment opportunities, serve the community, and establish a reimagined system.

According to Forbes Advisor, small businesses have made an astounding contribution to the job market, creating an astonishing 12.9 million employment opportunities over the past 25 years. The amazing reality is that you can be a contributor to that number and counting!

Now, there are definitely highs and lows of running a business. But from where I stand, after much trial and error, it has always been well worth the risk. There are practicals to consider but for the sake of mindset, it just takes one person to give thought to doing something differently. For us, we saw the holes in the childcare industry, considered the frustrations of what teachers and families were experiencing, and we focused on meeting those needs. We made a thoughtful effort to integrate what we observed in our surroundings and bring everything together. And along the way, we faced challenges in our business, experiencing significant financial losses and needing to adapt our approach. However, the revenue that came from our business allowed us to pay for the issues that arose from our business. If we had continued working for others as we did before, we would never have had the opportunity to generate such income or even experience substantial financial losses. It's important to recognize that businesses that lose millions of dollars daily would not have those dollars if the business itself didn't exist. Much of the process of running a business revolves around perspective. It begins with a spark of openness and a willingness to shift our mindset, giving ourselves the chance to break free from familiar cycles. To put it simply, it's a game. Those who are prepared to take bigger risks are also exposed to the the greatest rewards.

3

Four Sides To Business

"The best preparation for tomorrow is doing your best today."
-H. Jackson Brown, Jr., American Author

There are numerous business ideas available, but they can be categorized into four main types: brick and mortar, virtual/online, goods, and services. While most people tend to classify them as either brick-and-mortar or online, there are combinations that go beyond these two categories.

Virtual businesses offer the convenience of staying at home, avoiding travel hassles, browsing through inventory, or interacting with people. On the other hand, brick-and-mortar establishments provide a sense of connection and a tangible experience of what the business has to offer. Goods are physical, touchable products, while services involve paying for someone else's skills. Some companies have both physical and online presence, while others rely on word-of-mouth, without a physical location, and provide services.

Understanding the different types of businesses is crucial. It's important to identify your interests and determine the desired monthly income. Performing research on the average earnings in your chosen field can provide valuable information for you. Keep in mind that while scaling up is possible, if the numbers seem too low for your longterm goals, it might be worth considering other options. It's important to maintain a realistic perspective. For instance, desiring to be a highly-paid teacher without pursuing a doctorate degree might not align with reality. However, opening your own school, employing other teachers, and generating significant income becomes more attainable.

If considering running a t-shirt business, consider both a reimagined way to run that type of business and flush out several other options. If none or most of those options don't fit your goals, it's okay to move on to another idea- give yourself permission to keep going. The goal is to train yourself to actually consider options so you stick with it during the high and low seasons, aware of the success it can have.

I also want to take a quick moment to address those who are in urgent need of money. While chapter 5 provides some ideas for generating immediate income, I don't recommend this way of beginning this new chapter of your life. I'd rather suggest selling personal belongings, seeking donations from family and friends, or taking on temporary gigs to make what you need at the moment. The focus should be on getting out of these dire circumstances and not relying on quick money opportunities for long-term financial stability. Remember, we are working on changing our mindset. As a business owner, one of the perks is being able to create something that takes away the constant stress of just surviving.

In the beginning, my husband and I were in dire need of money, but we made a plan beforehand on how we could afford our living until the business grew, providing steady income. I highly recommend this approach because not all ideas will work out, and that's okay. It's all part of the journey. Once you achieve the success you're building towards, you will have the resilience and character to maintain it.

What type of business would bring you joy in building?

Will this business be based off of what you *need* at the moment or what you actually *want* to build? There is no wrong answer for this but make sure you know the honest answer before you start building.

4

Business Basics

"The journey of a thousand miles begins with one step."
-Lao Tzu, Chinese Philosopher and Writer

I hope you're feeling excited about the ideas you might have! If you find it overwhelming, but still have the desire to start your own business, I've included a list of businesses in the last chapter of this book. But before diving into building your business, it's important to have a solid idea of what you want to do. I've seen people struggle when their business keeps changing, and it becomes ineffective and stressful. I urge you not to fall into this trap, as it can be discouraging and impact your health and family. Take some time to research examples of businesses similar to your idea, and make note of what you love about them and what you would improve.

Now, let's quickly go over some business basics. There are different structures to consider:

- **Sole Proprietorship**: This is a business owned and operated by one individual. The owner is responsible for all the business's profits, losses, and liabilities.

- **Partnership**: A business where two or more individuals share ownership. Each partner contributes to the business and shares in its profits and losses.
- **Corporation**: A separate legal entity from its owners. It can generate profit, be taxed, and be held legally liable.
- **Limited Liability Company (LLC)**: A hybrid structure that combines the simplicity of a partnership with the liability protection of a corporation. Owners are not personally responsible for the company's debts or liabilities.
- **Nonprofit Organization**: A business whose primary goal is to benefit the public rather than making a profit. They are often involved in charitable, educational, or social activities.
- **Cooperative (Co-op)**: A business owned by the people who use its services. It is managed and controlled by its members, who have equal voting rights.

If you're new to opening your own business, I personally (not legally) recommend starting as a sole proprietor or forming a partnership if you have someone with you. Corporations and other organizations come with legal responsibilities, so it's important to gain some experience before taking on additional tax responsibilities, costs, and paperwork. However, once you get the hang of your business, it's crucial to seek legal advice from a professional to ensure you always operate with excellence.

One of the key benefits of owning your own business is the freedom to work for yourself. Moreover, there are potential tax advantages that come along with it. Here are some strategies to maximize tax deductions:

- **Home Office Deduction**: If you have a dedicated space in your home used exclusively for business, you may qualify to deduct certain home expenses such as rent/mortgage, mortgage interest, insurance, utilities, repairs, and depreciation.

- **Office Supplies**: The cost of office supplies used for business purposes in your home office can be deducted.
- **Utilities**: If you use a part of your home exclusively for business, a portion of your utility bills can potentially be deducted.
- **Phone and Internet Expenses**: If your phone and internet services are used for business purposes, you can deduct a proportionate part of the expense.
- **Property Taxes and Mortgage Interest**: Both property taxes and mortgage interest can be deducted, but only for the portion of your home used for business.
- **Repairs and Maintenance**: If repairs or maintenance are specific to the business area of your home, these expenses can be fully deducted. If they benefit your entire home, you can deduct the percentage that represents the proportion of your home used for business.
- **Depreciation**: If you own your home, you may be able to deduct the cost of wear and tear on the part of your home used for business. This is calculated based on the cost of your home and the percentage of your home used for business.
- **Meals**: Certain business-related meals are eligible for complete tax deduction. Remember to keep your receipts for proper record keeping. There are also convenient apps available that eliminate to need to keep paper receipts.

In my case, when we operated a childcare business in our house, we structured it so that only our bedroom and personal bathroom were exclusively used by us. The remaining areas of our house were utilized for the business, and we were able to claim the majority of it as tax deductions. We conducted thorough research and learned that by organizing our house in a certain way, we could take advantage of this opportunity, which proved successful. So, I encourage you to research how others have set up their homes or workspace to optimize their business and tax benefits.

Just keep in mind that once you start earning income, it's important to set aside an amount for taxes to be paid to the IRS or your country's tax service. When taxes are due, you might even receive a tax return if you have a long list of deductions.

The great news is that you will be working for yourself, providing job security and the satisfaction of building something you love. Previously, I worked for someone else, earning less than $3K per month. That was decent for a young adult but not enough to build a life with great balance. However, after starting our own business, we were able to earn over 3 times that amount, even after deducting expenses such as payroll, supplies, and food. Realizing the power of running your own business opened up endless possibilities for me.

If you have an interest in technology but lack expertise in certain areas required by the industry, you can still establish a tech company by offering a service and hiring individuals who possess the necessary knowledge. This way, you can surround yourself with what you love without investing significant time and money to learn unnecessary skills as a business owner. One of my favorite success stories is that of Rachael Ray, the American cook who dominated the food network and cookbooks all across the country. She is an author and TV personality with a network of $60 million dollars. Not only did she never finish college but she wasn't even trained in the culinary arts! I hope you're getting the point that anything is possible when it comes to owning a business.

What are you passionate about?

Are you willing to take a leap and explore new possibilities?

Depending on your state, there may be specific forms to fill out, but the process is usually straightforward. The Small Business Administration (SBA) provides valuable information on how to establish your business step-by-step, including resources for funding if needed. For now, the focus should be to allow yourself to think outside of what society has trained us to think, working for others, being led to just fill in the circle. Now you get to be the creator of your own circle- no better time than now!

5

What It Takes To Last

"Leadership is a combination of strategy and character. If you must be without one, be without the strategy."
-U.S. Gen. H. Norman Schwarzkopf

Owning a business provides a unique opportunity to discover the depth of your character. It unveils traits like ambition, laziness, passion, discipline, and balance. Unlike having a boss, there won't be someone guiding you on what to do and when to do it. Your success and financial gain will solely rely on your personal efforts. If you don't take action, your business won't thrive - for better or worse. The exciting part is that your dedication and hard work play a significant role in your achievements. Of course, external factors like market conditions and employment landscape matter, especially if you plan to expand your team. However, beyond that, the key lies in assembling something you're genuinely passionate about or believe will be successful, sharing your vision with others, and providing a product or service that meets their needs and desires.

This year, I decided that the business I had built for the last seven years, at which point brought in about a million per year, was not for me anymore. I knew that we could build an empire with it but it no longer brought me joy. I wasn't in the industry that I could look back years later and love my life. So my husband and I have decided to pivot. We took a huge pay cut but we are now rebranding and thinking of creative ways to build this new service. As I look back on the last seven years, it brought in around $144K of revenue in the first year to around 1 million on average the last few years. I think I did a great job for my first real business! I'm also incredibly grateful that my husband took the initiative to establish our business. He not only handled the majority of the legal aspects but continues to oversee that side of the corporation. It truly takes a special person to assume those responsibilities, as they don't bring me any joy. While setting up the business isn't overly complex, it does require focus and time to ensure everything is done properly. That's why I suggest starting as a sole proprietor or partner until you become more familiar with your business, your brand, or can afford legal counsel.

During my younger years, I offered dance classes in 8-week sessions to children ranging from five years old to high school age. At the end of each 8-week period, we would showcase the students' talents in a live performance for their families and friends. This business proved to be very rewarding for me, especially considering that, prior to this time, I had never received formal dance training aside from a single class in high school.

Even before that, I discovered a great opportunity while in high school. I realized that I could charge $4 per hour, per child, for my babysitting services. I made sure to target neighbors with multiple children. For instance, if someone had three children, they would pay me $12 per hour, which was significantly higher than what I earned working at coffee shops or retail stores. Moreover, I was able to keep all the profits at the time.

These experiences taught me the importance of character and the ability to think creatively. By pursuing activities that brought me joy and were worth my time, I was able to learn how to take care of myself, and eventually how to provide opportunities for my family.

If you're anything like me, you might not have always had the best character in certain aspects - and that's okay! A great starting point is to ask yourself the reason behind wanting to own your own business, or to question the motivations behind anything you do. When someone truly believes in what they're doing, enjoys it, recognizes the need for it, or does it for someone they love, they become more effective.

Personally, I realized the importance of surrounding myself with individuals whom I respected. I found inspiration in their life choices, faith, dedication, and observed how they handled various situations. I began to imitate their positive qualities. One word that eventually emerged and greatly impacted my journey is "diligence". Remember this word and let it take root in your mind and heart.

According to Google, diligence is "careful and persistent work or effort." This word has changed so much of who I am. When I think about the type of life I desire to have, the type of traits I want to be known for, I realize that diligence has become one of my best friends. There are days where it doesn't make sense to keep building business and character, when results don't come out as planned. But just enough consistency and there is a universal law that a profit will come about if you persist. Consider some ridiculous businesses or ideas out there that have made insane amounts of money. It doesn't matter what the majority of society thinks of them. Because they are persistent, they work! Their niche audience eventually finds them and they reward their *careful and persistent work or effort*. Whatever you choose to do, adopt this concept, hold it near and dear to you, pray about it, meditate on it, talk about it with others, whatever you need to embrace it, and watch what you build continue to blossom. You can do it, it's waiting for you!

Another word or concept to embrace is "mental fortitude." I only heard of this phrase within the last year or two and it is something that I pray for regularly, for myself and others. Entrepreneur.com says that mental fortitude "is defined as the ability to focus on and execute solutions when in the face of uncertainty or adversity." Having mental fortitude requires patience, endurance, and the ability to value the process as oppose to focusing mainly on the goal. Prematurely abandoning something often leads to missing out on the fruitful results that can be achieved through perseverance and commitment. The Global Entreneurship Monitor (G.E.M), holds an annual study on the effects of fear of failure when it comes to entrepreneurship. In 2022, 46% of Americans recognized the potential for starting their own business. Even 66% of these individuals believed they possessed the necessary skills to go after these opportunities. However, and sadly, 43% of the initial 46% decided to not pursue the business opportunity they saw, solely because of fear of failure. When you consider this statistic, it's truly disheartening. In a simplified breakdown, picture a group of 100 adults aged 18 to 64. Out of these, 46 see a promising business opportunity, and 30 of them possess the necessary skills to start and run a business. However, only 3 individuals take the leap of faith and overcome their fear of failure. These courageous few embrace diligence and mental fortitude as they pursue their passion. This kind of determination is truly powerful! What's even more remarkable is that you (yes, you!) have the potential to be one of those brave souls who create a small business, creating new avenues of income for yourself and others.

Do you see an opportunity to start your own business? Take the time to fully develop your idea by writing it out. Additionally, make sure to research nearby or similar businesses to determine the prices they charge for their products or services.

What is the biggest fear you have about starting your own business? If it's any encouragement, the economy wants to support small businesses so much, they offer tax perks, restart programs, and so much more.

6

Dream & Scheme

"All hard work brings a profit, but mere talk leads only to poverty."
-Proverbs 14:23, The Holy Bible

H aving covered the foundational mindset and business basics, I'm excited to share my favorite part - inspiring business ideas that ignite your mind, touch your heart, and possibly transform your life! While most people keep their ideas to themselves, I find myself constantly brainstorming new business ideas almost. And I want to share them with you, not only to clear my mind, but also to support your success if any of them resonate with you. Each category features around ten ideas, with some of them overlapping between categories. Let the creative sparks fly!

Brick-and-mortar:

- Set up a health drink/smoothie truck outside a gym, whether it's in their parking lot or conveniently located nearby. Offer a variety of healthy flavors to ensure consistency without spreading yourself too thin. Research the going rate for these drinks in your area, and consider increasing the price since you're catering to health-conscious individuals who value the convenience of having it readily available when they need it most.

- Setting up a coffee shop within a garden store or outdoor nursery is a brilliant idea. By renting a small space from the owner, you can keep your setup costs low while providing customers with the opportunity to enjoy nature. This unique combination not only benefits your own business but also supports another small business. Similarly, a coffee shop combined with a game store or a similar concept can create a fun and engaging experience for customers. These innovative combinations, like a library coffee shop, have a special charm that inspires people. It's as if customers feel they're getting two experiences for the price of one. This approach sets you apart and increases the likelihood of building an amazing reputation. To ensure success, focus on delivering exceptional value. This means serving high-quality coffee, curating great books, and creating a welcoming space where people can enjoy their time alone or with others. By providing customers with an overjoyed experience, you'll create a strong desire for them to return and spread the word!

- Transform your garage or a room in your home into a creative rental space, charging by the hour. As your business expands, you can branch out to other locations and offerings. Consider renting out an entire house, adorning each room with unique themes, and monetizing them hourly. Create a user-friendly booking website to streamline reservations. I know a family that currently manages seven small spaces, and they're not even in a bustling city. If you reside in a major metropolis, the potential for generating income through this avenue is even higher. The beauty of this idea is that it can be a lucrative side gig, not requiring full-time commitment.

- Establish a child care cafe where parents can safely leave their children to play under supervision, affording them time to focus on their work. This concept is a winner! Offering monthly memberships to parents for utilizing this service can be a great way to generate consistent revenue. You can even charge based on what membership package they sign up for (two or four hours per day). The play area can be simple yet engaging, or you can go all out with innovative features. After all, entertaining children is not as complicated as it may seem. You can even incorporate a meal, educational activities, crafts, and plenty of interactive playtime.
- Explore opportunities in the pet industry, such as veterinary services, pet grooming, or pet food delivery. You can even consider operating a mobile pet cleaning service, visiting clients' homes in a specially equipped van.
- A visit to a music store can be an enjoyable experience, although with the abundance of free and online music, it's important to offer something unique like live performances. Again, customers will feel like they are getting the value of two experiences for the price of one. Placing the entire concept in a laundromat could potentially attract enough attention to be featured in a news article. With customers typically spending nearly two hours waiting for their clothes, they would have ample time to explore the music and even enjoy live performances. This arrangement presents a mutually beneficial opportunity that is hard to overlook.
- A dance club that caters to a unique audience. Many people have ditched the usual night scene but they are always looking for unique and safe experiences. I recently heard of a couple that opened a dance club that played Christian themed dance music, which is genius. That can be applied to really any niche audience and you're good to go.
- A fantastic way to create a brick-and-mortar presence without com-

mitting to a long-term contract is by hosting a pop-up business. By applying these principles to a pop-up, you'll create an exhilarating experience for those in the neighborhood who have the opportunity to visit your shop or event. The versatility of pop-ups allows you to choose various locations, such as inside a building, on a curb, in a park, or even a parking lot. Whether you're selling goods or providing services, the possibilities are endless.

- There are a variety of food stores available, including health food stores, butcher shops, and specialty stores catering to specific dietary preferences such as vegan or keto options.

- A gaming store or mobile truck offers an exciting experience for both young and old. I recently came across a mobile truck equipped with multiple screens and game controls. It was fascinating! People of all ages eagerly waited for their turn to join in on the gaming action. Renting this truck by the hour for events is a brilliant way to engage with a wide and enthusiastic audience. Whether you opt for a stationary building or a mobile setup, the key lies in creating an unforgettable experience. And the best part? It doesn't have to break the bank. By searching for bargains on screens, controllers, and other necessary items, you can keep the costs manageable while still delivering exciting entertainment.

Virtual:

- Digital products can be highly lucrative for online businesses. Within this realm, various ideas flourish, including audio books, e-books, online graphics, and online courses. It's inspiring to witness educators creating and selling their educational materials to fellow teachers. This market has experienced significant growth in the post-pandemic era, with the rise of online education.

- Offering website design services doesn't require coding knowledge.

Years ago, I provided my services to small businesses without websites. I created different packages for them to choose from. Fresh out of college and in need of money, I took on the challenge despite lacking formal training. I charged a competitive rate, confident that I could deliver their desired online presence. For a basic site, I charged $500, which I could build within a couple of hours using an online platform. Alternatively, I offered a more comprehensive package for $1000, which included on-site photography and videos. Realizing that many businesses lacked the know-how to maintain their websites, I started offering a monthly fee for updates. Nowadays, with a keen eye and captivating designs, someone can even charge $5000 for a small business. Platforms like Wix, Squarespace, Web.com, Shopify, and many others offer free or low-cost options.

- Dropshipping! It's an exciting and cost-effective business, but it does require some time to learn, and the industry is highly competitive. However, to be frank, even in a saturated market, there are often ample opportunities to generate income.
- An online administrative program may appear saturated in the post-COVID-19 era of stay-at-home measures. However, starting with friends or local small businesses increases your chances of gaining trust compared to a random person from a distant location. Moreover, offering services that larger companies don't provide significantly enhances your chances of being prioritized.
- Affiliate marketing serves as the vital bridge connecting manufacturers or brands to their consumers. While many businesses opt for social media, there are other avenues worth exploring. Regardless of your choice, this method offers a fantastic opportunity to generate income without the hassle of storing inventory or creating products.
- E-commerce is a wild beast in the online space. This concept revolves around providing utmost convenience to consumers.

Essentially, it functions as a global online store, eliminating the need for physical retail spaces and allowing seamless integration with e-commerce to avoid inventory management. It caters to a wide range of industries, including beauty, fashion, retail, stationary, and even digital products, as we previously discussed.

- A virtual assistant goes beyond traditional in-person assistance, providing support for various virtual needs. From managing emails to tackling complex tasks, the level of assistance depends on your specific skill set and abilities.

- As an app developer, I may not have the expertise on this matter, but I've heard from a few friends who have had success with outsourcing app development to professionals from different countries at a significantly lower cost. There are certainly ways to acquire the skills needed to create your own app or develop apps for others through online courses that are either free or more affordable compared to returning to school.

- Domain investing! I recently learned about this and purchased a few domains myself (four to be exact). Essentially, you search for domains that others may be interested in purchasing in the future. For instance, if I reside in Los Angeles and know that there is a thriving community of dancers in the area, I can brainstorm a domain name that could attract someone's attention. Let's take "dancersofLA.com" as an example. I can acquire it for just $1 and become the owner. Now, imagine if I come up with a list of domain names and purchase a hundred of them, each costing $1. In total, I would have spent $100. With this collection of domains, I can reach out to local businesses, influencers, and individuals who might be interested in buying a domain at a much higher price. Let me share another example that I find fascinating. Suppose I own a coffee shop on Main Street and someone approaches me with an offer to sell their domain, such as coffeeonmain.com or coffeeonmainst.com, for $100. This presents a fantastic opportunity for both parties involved. I get to have a website name that perfectly aligns with my business, attracting more traffic, while the seller receives a significant return on their investment, going from $1 to $100 for a single domain.

- YouTube is a well-known avenue for generating income, but it requires time and consistent effort. However, if you're dedicated to growing your channel and if both you and your audience find the content intriguing, it's definitely worth your while.

Service:

- Offer a house cleaning service where households pay a monthly fee. You can hire individuals, like friends or family, to work by the hour and keep the profits without needing to clean yourself.
- Print on demand is something that you can really enjoy if you are like to be creative. Many people don't know how to print or what it takes to get their products printed. Many people struggle with the printing process and don't know where to start. Differentiate yourself by offering something unique that competitors don't. Here's a hint: Find a way to continue the relationship so they will always come back to you. You can help create a logo for them and offer it on multiple items. They'll always look to you for their event merchandise needs.
- Other notable businesses worth mentioning include dog walking, party planning, event coordination, and hairstyling.
- Freelance writing and blogging can be a lucrative side hustle. However, if you're passionate about writing, there are incredible opportunities to build a successful career in this field. You don't even have to be the writer yourself. Start your own writing business and hire talented writers based on project requirements. Plus, with

the help of artificial intelligence, providing high-quality writing becomes effortless. Simply provide the AI platform with directions, and it will deliver outstanding content. The possibilities are endless.

- Elderly care. This is a beautiful option for the person that loves to take care of a valuable group of people. So many elderly living situations need much improvement on the quality of care they offer. Families will pay to have them live in a communal space that takes great care of their parents or elderly family members.

- Photography. Do your own research for your area but photographers can make a ton of money! There is a photography business that even owns a truck that drives around offering headshots in busy areas. Depending on your area, research what type of photography is needed. You can offer seasonal deals, depending on the upcoming holiday, and even have your consistent clientele. There will always be someone birthday, wedding, funeral, job party, holiday party, monumental family phase that needs to be captured.

- Short-term rental hosting has become an increasingly popular business these days, but there is still ample opportunity for newcomers! Not only are there various types of short-term rentals, but there are also mid-term rental options available. In fact, even hospitals are willing to pay for accommodations to house their traveling nurses for a few months.

- As a content creator, you have the opportunity to serve other businesses or create content for your own brand. What's great is that many businesses struggle with delivering high-quality content to their online audience. By leveraging your skills, you can help them overcome this challenge and provide valuable content that resonates with their target audience.

- A potential business idea is home decorating or home staging for properties that are being sold in the real estate market. I once had a neighbor who specialized in staging homes and would later sell the furniture used in the staging process. I found this idea to be brilliant. The real estate company would cover the cost of staging the house and wouldn't require the furniture once the house was sold. Additionally, as a home decorating business, there are numerous online resources available to teach design styles for inspiration. This means that even if you don't have exceptional decorating skills or lack confidence, you can still make a living. Many individuals simply prefer to rely on others to help them decorate their spaces.

- A landscaping business or anything to do with property maintenance will always be a need. I know people who have found great success in this type of venture. Once homeowners or property owners discover your reputation for exceptional maintenance, they'll have you on speed dial. Some people get such a good reputation, they have to start hiring other people to cover their contracts. Even if you find this not to be your specialty, this type of business is still attainable. It is possible to venture into the landscaping or handyman business even without prior experience in the industry. As long as you have a reliable network of one or two individuals to call upon when you secure a job, you can compensate them on an hourly basis and charge a higher fee to the client, thereby generating profit for yourself.

- Live performances are a must for all entertainers out there. At some point, everyone will crave entertainment at their event. Much of the growth in this industry comes from word of mouth, and if you're talented, you'll always be in demand. I'll never forget the time I performed at a show alongside an up-and-coming artist who got paid a whopping $20,000 for just 15 minutes on stage. It blew my mind! Weddings, birthday parties, funerals, festivals - they all require someone to captivate the audience with their talent. A wedding band, for example, can easily earn an average of $5,000 for a few hours of work (that's about $1,000 per band member). And if a singer or band is touring and performing at a venue that holds 1,000 people with tickets priced at $20 each, the potential earnings reach $20,000. If you have a contract that guarantees you 75% or more of the ticket sales, you can take home at least $15,000! If this is your passion, we need more exceptional talent out there, so don't hesitate to give it your all. And let's not forget about online music sales and social media views - especially if you have a dedicated YouTube following. But even if you don't, it's still worth your time and effort.

Goods:

- Floral and plant shops never lose their charm! What's exciting about these establishments is the opportunity to expand beyond a brick-and-mortar store. By offering additional services, like collaborating with websites or local event venues, you can cultivate essential relationships that generate extra income for your business. Sharing the beauty of nature with others, through inspiring aesthetics and captivating fragrances, is truly special. Some shops successfully operate both online and offline, raking in monthly revenues ranging from 10K to over 100K, depending on location and strategic setup. If you offer delivery services, revenue potential can skyrocket, but it's crucial to plan for logistics like delivery trucks or partnering with a reliable delivery service. Ensuring the freshness of the florals during shipping is also super important, and secure packaging can simplify handling. Moreover, selling live plants instead of cut flowers enhances their lifespan during transportation and post-delivery. The success of floral companies in today's market makes my heart very happy.
- Candle-making is a delightful business to pursue. It offers the

convenience of being a go-to gift option, while also being relatively low-cost depending on the quality and sourcing. If you're involved in crafting the candles yourself, it's important to consider the time investment. However, many companies offer bulk purchases at affordable prices. By adding an eye-catching front sticker and elegant packaging, this presents a wonderful opportunity to generate additional income. With the potential to go beyond just additional income, if you reimagine this business idea, it can become a full-fledged career and corporation. Candles have a unique ability to bring comfort, making them an ideal product to build a solid brand around. It's important to understand what sets your company apart and how it makes people feel when they light that candle. For those who are passionate about these ideas and willing to put in the effort, there is immense potential for success.

- Speaking of candles, a great idea is to sell gift baskets with a few items that go together, and you can make it personal. These types of businesses can do so well because it's provides a service that connect people to others. This can be a brick-and-mortar and a virtual option.

- Buying and reselling from returned pallets is a fascinating business idea that has recently caught my attention. I am truly captivated by the concept, although it is crucial to consider storage options for the purchased items until they are sold. Thankfully, there are direct liquidation sites and even Facebook groups dedicated to these incredible deals. However, it is important to acknowledge the element of uncertainty in this type of business. When it comes to pallets, the unknown awaits with hidden treasures or even peculiar items that may be challenging to resell. However, the true appeal lies in the fact that pallets can be obtained for as little as a few hundred dollars, making it an exceptionally cost-effective endeavor to begin.

- One possibility is to create your own juice and sell it at events, with the potential to secure a contract with a larger store. While coffee roasters excel in this area, there is also an opportunity to achieve success with a homemade beverage.
- Pop-up shops offer a curated selection of unique items tailored to the interests of the local community.
- Selling baked goods, whether online or in-person, offers various opportunities. You can establish a fixed location or operate from a mobile cart. Another exciting option is to target regular businesses as your customers. By creating contracts with them, you can plan the quantity and frequency of deliveries. This approach has significant growth potential, especially if you establish strong and consistent relationships with companies.
- Creating beauty products, particularly those made with natural and healthy ingredients, is a passion that resonates with people. These sought-after goods enhance the quality of their lives and provide a sense of uniqueness.
- I have developed a love for stationary and my collection seems to be growing uncontrollably. Creating cards is one of my favorite activities in this realm, and if you take advantage of in-person opportunities, many people are enthusiastic about supporting these types of businesses. Nowadays, a single card can cost as much as $6. However, if it features an exceptional or humorous message or design, people are willing to invest in something that helps them connect with their loved ones. Additionally, you can complement this venture with other stationary items such as notebooks, pens, stickers (yay!), calendars, drawing pads, and gift bags.
- Flipping furniture has stood the test of time and remains a timeless pursuit. One of my family members has shared so much about how successful this business has been for her. The process is simple: find discarded items on the street or at garage sales, give them a

thorough clean, stain if needed, and resell them for a significant profit - sometimes even multiplying the original purchase price by ten or one hundred times. With a simple set of tools, this affordable venture offers an incredible opportunity to kickstart a business.

7

Conclusion

I always encourage business memberships as they provide a steady stream of income compared to one-time customers. Remember, despite the saturation of businesses, there is still ample room for more! Only a small percentage of people seize the opportunity, while the majority remain consumers. It has been a pleasure sharing ideas with you and I appreciate your attentive listening.

What are the top 3 ideas that stuck out most to you?

It's time to carve out dedicated time in our weekly schedule to embark on the building process. Be sure to mark it in our calendar and share it with someone who can provide support and hold you accountable as you take the first steps towards building- I'm so excited for you!

You have the potential to join the small percentage of individuals who overcome the fear of failure. Embracing the necessary traits not only benefits your income, but also enhances your overall life. As a business owner, witnessing the impact on clients, employees, and the community is truly rewarding.

Finally, this marks the debut of my very first book, and I would deeply appreciate a review on how it has influenced your perspective on embarking on your own business or any inspiration it may have sparked in your life. Here's to a new chapter and an exciting journey ahead!